MANITOBA

MANITOBA

Photographs by Robert Taylor

Introduction by Fred McGuinness

Toronto
OXFORD UNIVERSITY PRESS
1981

Plate 12 is reproduced by kind permission of the Royal Winnipeg Ballet.

Plates 60 and 61 are reproduced by kind permission of the Hudson Bay Mining and Smelting Co., Ltd. Flin Flon, Manitoba.

Designed by Fortunato Aglialoro
©Oxford University Press (Canadian Branch) 1981
ISBN 0-19-540341-X
1 2 3 4—4 3 2 1
Printed in Hong Kong by
EVERBEST PRINTING COMPANY LIMITED

INTRODUCTION
by Fred McGuinness

In geography and climate Manitoba closely resembles Alberta and Saskatchewan, its sister provinces—they are called collectively the Prairie Provinces—but the social history of Manitoba is markedly different.

As early as 1612 Thomas Button sailed through Hudson Strait and explored the west coast of Hudson Bay. Half a century later, in 1668, one tiny ketch, the *Nonsuch*, returned from the Bay with a fabulous cargo of luxurious furs that excited all of Europe. Englishmen who had formerly sought to invest in the silks and spices of Cathay now realized there was a profit to be made in beaver skins. Two years after that historic voyage, in 1670, the world first heard of the 'Company of Adventurers of England trading into Hudson's Bay'. Receiving title to 'Rupert's Land'—the drainage basin of Hudson Bay extending as far west as the valley of the Saskatchewan—the Hudson's Bay Company built posts on Hudson Bay and James Bay, inducing the Indians to trade there, unlike rival French fur traders from Montreal who went into the interior to meet the Indians. In the course of the 1730s the explorer La Vérendrye and his *voyageurs* established two western supply posts: Fort La Reine, on the present site of Portage la Prairie, and Fort Rouge at the junction of the Red and Assiniboine Rivers, on the present site of Winnipeg.

Many of the explorers and fur traders from Quebec took Indian women as wives, and the children of these marriages became known as Métis—people of mixed blood. After the fall of New France in 1759 the French fur trade passed into the hands of English, Scottish, and American merchants who had moved into Montreal and eventually formed the North West Company. The Métis, who were superb horsemen and highly skilled buffalo hunters, served the traders of the North West Company well, supplying them with pemmican. Thus they became tools in the struggle for control of the western fur trade between the North West Company of Montreal and the British Hudson's Bay Company.

In 1812 the Hudson's Bay Company granted Lord Selkirk 116,000 square miles of land (Assiniboia), and at the junction of the Red and Assiniboine Rivers he established a settlement that was colonized by a party of Scots and Irish crofters who had made their way in York boats southward from Port Churchill on Hudson Bay. Somehow they survived drought, flood, famine, and rival traders to establish the Red River Settlement, bringing white society and agriculture to the Great Plains.

Strategically located in the area from which the North West Company drew pemmican, and across which it brought supplies to its upper posts, the Red River Settlement was seen by the Nor'Westers as a threat to their business. They encouraged the Métis to feel that the Red River settlers were robbing them of their land and threatening their historic rights and patterns of livelihood. This led to several confrontations between the settlers and the Métis, in one of which, the Battle of Seven Oaks in June 1816, Governor Robert Semple and twenty settlers and Hudson's Bay Company men were killed by Métis led by Cuthbert Grant, himself of mixed blood but English-speaking.

Métis resentments grew, even after the two companies united in 1821—particularly when it was learned in 1857 that the Province of Canada was making plans to acquire the Northwest. In 1869 a team of surveyors arrived in the Red River area. Louis Riel, leader of the Métis, issued a direct challenge to them, convinced that the Canadian government had no right to make surveys on Métis lands without permission of the Settlement. Riel stood on the surveyors' chain and told them to stop. His words were bold: 'This far and no farther.' Riel's further acts of resistance, his capture of Fort Garry in November 1869 and the formation of a Provisional Government, his insistence on the death by firing-squad of Thomas Scott in March 1870, and his flight to Pembina across the American border in August are well known. Though his actions were misguided, their consequences for the West were immense. In March 1870 a Bill of Rights proposed by Riel was sent to Ottawa, and it influenced the formulation of the Manitoba Act, passed by Parliament in May, under which Red River would enter Confederation as a province. The transcontinental destiny of the young Confederation was now assured. Louis Riel was filled with ambiguities and contradictions; in his own time he inspired hatred and idolatry, admiration and contempt. But he has with reason been called the Father of Manitoba. Today he lies buried almost in the shadow of St Boniface Cathedral.

The Red River is not only at the centre of Manitoba history; its valley is the cradle of the Prairies. Along its banks the first settlers grew grain that gave promise to the endless acres that lay to the west. And it was up the Red River in 1867 that an enterprising seed merchant shipped to eastern markets the first load of 'Manitoba No. 1 Northern'—the red-gold wheat that became the standard against which all other wheats would be measured. That first bargeload of only 867 bushels led the way for billions more to follow. The success of Manitoba as a producer of grain and livestock was best foretold in a line from a letter home to Scotland written by one of Lord Selkirk's party: 'The plow, from the first, met with no obstruction, and the soil proved in the highest degree rich and productive.'

Demarcation of the plains into sections and townships opened the empty acres of Manitoba to a flood of newcomers. A hundred years later, great-grandchildren still remain faithful to the land, and in addition to traditional crops can now plant rapeseed and triticale, both of which were developed at the University of Manitoba. Their capital city, Winnipeg, now a major centre of the world's grain trade, bears strong evidence of the golden commodity on which it was founded. Grain is the basis of an economy that provides services for all of the Canadian West, and its influence is everywhere. Numerous boards, commissions, faculties, and councils buy it, research it, and move it to market. It even provided the title for a fine novel.*

Grain brought to Manitoba people who, in establishing a new society, kept alive the cultures and traditions of their many homelands. For their communities they chose distinc-

Grain (1926) by Robert Stead.

tive names that a century later remain an integral part of the mosaic of Manitoba. Aubigny, Ile des Chénes, and Ste Rose du Lac mark the French influence; Steinbach, Altona, and Blumenort the influence of German Mennonites. The Scots named Selkirk, Angusville, Clanwilliam, and Glencairn. Lonely Icelanders, wanting to feel more at home, named their fishing villages Gimli, Lundar, and Reykjavik. Deloraine was settled and named by a colony of Belgians, and the French-named Dauphin became the Ukrainian capital of Canada. Each of these different communities has woven its own threads in the historic tapestry of Manitoba.

The city of Brandon, the major community on the principal east-west waterway, the Assiniboine River, was called 'The Wheat City' by early settlers because of its importance as a grain-shipping centre. Today it is hard to imagine that fleets of *voyageurs* with canoes filled with furs navigated this tortuous stream, and almost inconceivable that before the CPR, sidewheelers and paddlewheelers delivered trade goods and settlers' effects as far west as the Saskatchewan border.

Major developments are taking place in the north where Manitoba's history began. It is here that engineers and builders are creating brand-new towns to serve the enormous mines and hydro installations. In the midst of development, however, Manitobans still cherish their heritage of flora and fauna. Fenceposts along endless miles of country roads bear thousands of nesting boxes for visiting birds, and each spring and autumn naturalists gather from all over Canada to watch their migrations.

Manitoba is rich in culture as well as in natural beauty and resources. This is demonstrated by hundreds of fine museums and private collections, and by each summer's series of ethnic festivals. Ukrainians celebrate at Dauphin and Gardenton, Indians at The Pas, Icelanders at Gimli, the French at St Boniface, and all celebrate together at Winnipeg. Literature has also flourished. Such diverse and important writers as Ernest Thompson Seton, Robert Stead, Frederick Philip Grove, Laura Goodman Salverson, W.L. Morton, Gabrielle Roy, Margaret Laurence, and W.D. Valgardson have established a prolific literary tradition. Manitobans have music and ballet of world calibre. The Winnipeg Symphony and the internationally famous Royal Winnipeg Ballet are not for the élite alone but bring the finest of classical music and dance to the people. Finally, history is kept alive in Manitoba. Each summer trainloads of tourists scramble over the stoneworks of Fort Prince of Wales, near Churchill, where French and English fleets once fought for control of the fur trade.

In Manitoba one can see the striking contrasts between the old and the new. Thus it is that in the Interlake area the most modern combines harvest grain for export, while on a nearby lakeshore Indian families garner wild rice as their ancestors did. From eventful historic origins, from the courage of those who led the way, from the bounty of nature and the diversity of human imagination, Manitobans have created a remarkable province, the genesis of Canada's West.

1 Prairie crocus near Winnipeg

2 Spring stubble fires near Clandeboye
3 Dusty spring, near Deloraine

4 Snowshoe Hare, The Pas
5 Souris River in flood, near Souris

6 Moose, eastern Manitoba
7 Spruce forest, The Pas

8 Whitemouth
9 Kososki's General Store, Beauséjour

10 Portage and Main, Winnipeg
11 CP railyards, Winnipeg

12 Margaret Slota and Baxter Branstetter, Royal Winnipeg Ballet
summer open-air performance in Assiniboine Park.
13 Downtown Winnipeg by night, with the Legislative Building

14 The grave of Louis Riel, with St Boniface Cathedral, Winnipeg
15 The paddle-wheeler *Queen* cruising on the Red River at Winnipeg

16 Cattle crossing near Deloraine

17 The main street of Hartney

18 Coots on a prairie marsh, Kaleida
19 Beaver

20 Sailing into harbour, Hnausa
21 Harness racing, Glenboro

22 Souris
23 Cattle near Mountain Road

24 & 25 Harvesting wild rice, Pointe du Bois
a Wild rice, Whiteshell River
b Children collecting wild rice
c Checking the rice
d Bagging the rice

26 Old fishing-shed, Hecla
27 Fishing boats up for winter, Riverton

28 Catfish Creek Fishing-station,
Lake Winnipeg
29 a Fish drying and a fish smoker,
Catfish Creek
b Cabin and gear, Catfish Creek
c & d Macbeth fishing-station,
Lake Winnipeg

30 Railway station, Carman
31 Prairie Dog Central Railway,
Grosse Isle

32 Mennonite museum, Steinbach

33 Flea-market, Glenboro

34 Great gray owl (male, hooting), Spruce Siding

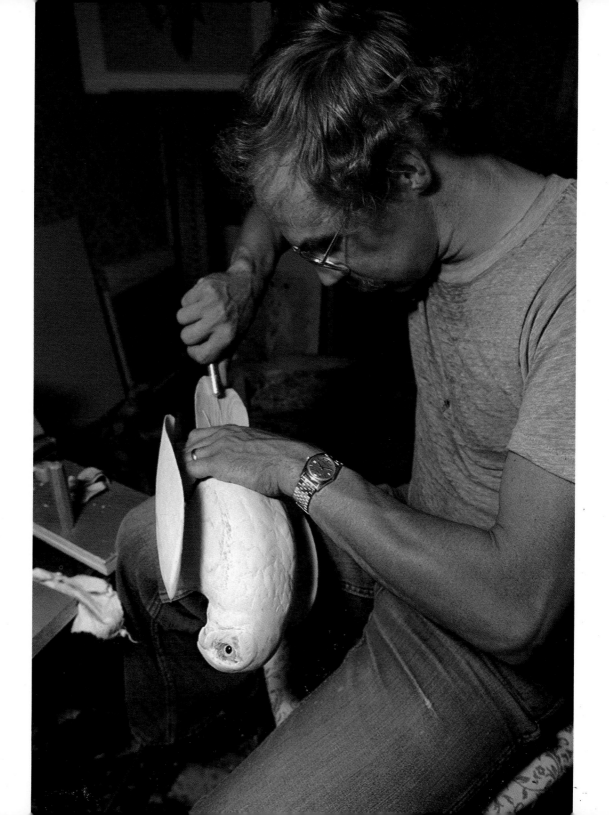

35 Peter Sawatzky, bird carver

36 Eli Kostenchuk repairing
church statues, Mountain Road
37 The Ruthenian Greek Catholic
Church of St John, Rackham

38 Fort Dauphin museum, Dauphin
39 Ukrainian dancers, Dauphin

40 Jack Mulvena in a Red River cart, Austin

41 Deloraine

42 Mrs Eli Kostenchuk, Mountain Road

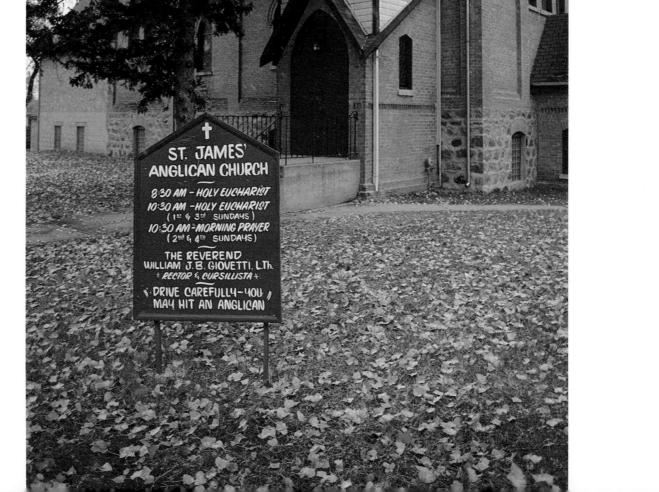

The sign reads:

ST. JAMES'
ANGLICAN CHURCH

8:30 AM — HOLY EUCHARIST
10:30 AM — HOLY EUCHARIST
(1st & 3rd SUNDAYS)
10:30 AM — MORNING PRAYER
(2nd & 4th SUNDAYS)

THE REVEREND
WILLIAM J. B. GIOVETTI, L.Th.
* RECTOR & CURSILLISTA *

DRIVE CAREFULLY—YOU
MAY HIT AN ANGLICAN

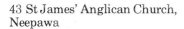

43 St James' Anglican Church,
Neepawa

44 White Admiral butterfly and
Sapsucker holes, Hecla Island
45 Bison, Riding Mountain
National Park

46 Old St Andrew's on the Red, south of Lockport
47 Swathing grain near Erickson

48 Least chipmunk, The Pas
49 Brandon

50 Stack-wall barn, north of Gimli
51 George Ball hoeing dandelions,
Rapid City

52 Falls at Seven Sisters
53 Crowduck portage, Whiteshell
Provincial Park

54 & 55 Portage la Prairie

56 Winter fun, Hazel Creek,
near Ste Rita

57 Autumn colours, Churchill

ᑯᐅᐳᖅᑉᐊᖅ ᐃᐅᐅᐃᑕ ᓄᐊᖅᕐᑕᐅ

ARMY SURPLUS · FURS BROUGHT AND SOLD · ESKIMO CARVINGS · TOURIST INFORMATION · OUTFITS FOR EXPLORERS · IVORY JEWELLE

58 Arctic Trading Company, Churchill

59 Fort Prince of Wales, Churchill

a

b

60 & 61 Hudson Bay Mining and
Smelting Plant, Flin Flon
a Smelter plant
b Scoop train in mine
c Mine tunnels
d Producing copper

c

d

62 Grain-ship leaving port, Churchill
63 Tide-stranded ice, Hudson Bay coast, Churchill

64 & 65 Polar bears, Gordon Point,
east of Churchill

66 Spruce trees and fog, Churchill
67 Shield-country lakes, Whiteshell Provincial Park

68 Getting water, Clearwater Lake, The Pas
69 Ice-crystals forming a sun-circle, Headingley

70 Cross-country skiers, Spruce Woods
71 Riding Mountain National Park

72 Ice sculptures, *Festival du Voyageur,* St Boniface
73 Sleigh ride, *Festival du Voyageur,* St Boniface

74 Daisies by the roadside, Whiteshell Provincial Park
75 Whiteshell River

76 Pigeons on a grain-elevator, Brandon
77 Combine-harvester on a highway, Whitemouth

78 Rackham
79 Snow geese, Oak-Hammock Marsh

80 Sunflowers near Ste Agathe